I0157051

Poetry N Motion

Personal Expressions of the Power, Grace, and Love of God

Sheila R. McElroy

Watercress Press 2014

PoetryNMotion
Copyright © 2014 by Sheila McElroy

Printed in the United States of America
ISBN-13: 978-0-9897822-9-6

A *Watercress Press* book
from Geron & Associates
www. watercresspress.com

Scripture quotations taken from the *New American Standard Bible*® Copyright © 1960,1962, 1968, 1971.1972.1973.1977, 1995 by the Lockman Foundation, used by permission. (www.Lockman.org)

Scripture quotations are taken from the Holy Bible, New Living Translation, copyright © 1996, 2004, 2007, 2013 by Tyndal House Foundation. Used by permission of Tyndale House Publishers, Inc., Carol Stream, Illinois 60188. All Rights reserved.

The Holy Bible, New International Version®, NIV® Copyright© 1973, 1978, 1984, 2011 by Biblica, Inc. ® Used by permission. All rights reserved worldwide.

The poem "The Lord is My Banner" was previously published in the anthology Invoking the Muse, published by the International Library of Poetry, and included here by permission of the publisher.

Photography: Sheila R. McElroy and 3iii Graphic Studios
Cover design: 3iii Graphic Studios

Acknowledgements

First, and above all, personal and intimate thanks go to my Lord, and Savior Jesus Christ, Who has made all things possible.

I am also grateful for numerous people who have given their love and support over the years. Special thanks to the following people:

- To my parents, *Aline T. Cannady* and *David McElroy*, and my stepfather, *Albert M. Cannady* for their undying love and support.
- To my siblings; Johnny, Robert, and Renaye (Naye-Naye) for being the best siblings a sister could have.
- To my nieces and nephews for always making 'Auntie Sheila' feel loved.
- To my uncles and aunts, John H. Taylor, Clara L. Beverly, and Hattie M. King, who always believed in me and encouraged me to pursue my goals.
- To my friend and mentor, Olga Samples Davis for her precious patience, love, caring heart, and spiritual guidance, which encouraged me to step out on faith.
- To both of my church families, Living Faith Community Church, and West End Baptist Church for their faithful and and continuous support.
- To Chaplains Miguel Albert and Mary Diehl for their unending spiritual guidance.
- Finally – to all my friends and co-workers (you know who you are) for your endless love, support, and encouragement throughout this journey.

God's blessings to each and every one of you!

Dedication

Above all, this book is dedicated to my Father in Heaven, who has loved me unconditionally since the beginning. Lord, I worship your Holy name, and fervently sing your praises. If it had not been for this poetic gift you have graciously given me, this book would not exist. So this compilation of poetry is about you, Lord. My life is about you – without you, life is meaningless. And so it is, I am grateful for the invitation and opportunity to develop a more personal and intimate relationship with you through poetry. My life is at peace because of you, Lord.

After the Lord, I would like to acknowledge the following people in this dedication:

To my wonderful mother, Aline – who always encouraged us to get an education. Her most "precious and priceless" educational gift of all was making sure her children knew Jesus. I love you for that, Mom.

To my beautiful aunt, Aunt Hattie – the one who always allowed me to be me, who laughed with me, listened to me, never judged me, and encouraged me to keep writing. Auntie, you are missed more than you know.

To the late Reverend A. Bernard Devers, former pastor of the West End Baptist Church, who through guidance of the Holy Spirit allowed God to use him to set forth the platform for the Lord to begin a work in me through presentational poetry. Thank you, Reverend D., for having a heart for God.

Poetry N Motion

Personal Expressions of the Power, Grace, and Love of God

Contents

Praise and Honor

Motivation and Spiritual Strength

Inspiration Through Spiritual Journeys

NOTES: Moments of Reflection & Conversations with God

Foreword

In the Biblical account of the story of creation, Genesis 1:3 states, *"And God said, let there be light: and there was light."* This passage points to the creative power of God — the One who is the first cause of all life, form and movement. God's Words have the ability to cause change and bring motion where there is only emptiness and lifelessness.

We've had the wonderful opportunity of seeing the Lord change lives by working through people and in all sorts of places. Yes, God speaks through the pulpit and preaching, but He is not limited by the vehicles or venues that we typically think. He speaks through mules as well as men and through praise as well as poetry.

Sheila McElroy serves as one of God's instruments by using her poetic gift to give motion to words; to bring fullness out of emptiness and life out of lifelessness. Her eclectic works from *PoetryNmotion* reflects imagery and rhyme flowing from a heart of faith, beating in the rhythm of God's grace and love. Hebrews 10:24 lets us know that we, the body of Christ, must continuously be in the business of *"spurring one another on toward love and good deeds."*

Over the past 12 years, Sheila has been led by the Holy Spirit to put "pen to paper" for the sole purpose of encouraging believers through spoken word while giving all glory to the Lord. In this, her first addition of poetic works, we get the chance to see the power of her speech in print form. Her gentle spirit, life experiences, hunger for the things of God, and willingness to venture out into deeper waters all serve to bring her to this moment in her life.

Sheila came into our lives just a short time ago, yet it feels like we have known her all of our lives. As a sister in Christ, we could immediately see her heart for God and her desire to reach His people through all that He has poured into her. One of her greatest joys is to take what the Holy Spirit has shared in her heart and deliver it into the hearing of the local congregation; all to edify the body and glorify God. We are grateful for the gift that the Lord has shared with Living Faith Community Church through Sheila.

The very heart of God is that people would come to know Him in a deep and intimate relationship. This book of poetry has the capacity to both challenge and inspire those who seek to walk in step with the Lord.

Blessings,
Pastor Kevin and Sister Jackie Love
Living Faith Community Church

A Word from the Author

When I think of God's unconditional, unending, and perfect love, it leads me to reflect on what Christian poetry means to me. For me, writing poetry began as a way to talk to God about my troubles. Today, it is about having a constant conversation with God, because I know that he has my absolute best interest at heart. I can tell him everything. This time with God also allows me to reflect on my youthful years and time spent with my grandmother, Rozina Taylor.

One day, while sitting next to her, I watched her every move and listened to her every word. I did this often simply because she was "Grandma" and I loved her dearly. On this particular day, I saw a picture of a woman on the wall.

I asked, "Grandma, who is that lady?"

She responded, "That is Mahalia Jackson."

I said, "Who is Mahalia Jackson?"

Grandma replied, "The greatest gospel singer in the world." She then instructed me to play Mahalia's gospel album. I liked what I heard. Even as a child, it did something to me. One of my favorite songs to this day is, "Come on Children, Let's Sing." Singing this song often reminds me of why I write Christian poetry; I can sing God's praises and shout all about His goodness and everlasting love. Through poetry I can spread the Gospel of Jesus Christ and share His love – the love that lives within me. God's BOUNTIFUL GRACE, MERCY, and GOODNESS soothes my soul – my cup runs over.

The Father has given each of us gifts. We are all representatives of the Kingdom of God and should share our gifts with each other. May my gift of poetry penetrate your heart, and lead you towards developing a more personal and intimate relationship with the Master. All you have to do is talk to Him . . . talk to Him! Represent Him in all you do so that your gift may become a light for others. He welcomes us into this intimate relationship and invites us to experience an extraordinary kind of love.

Praise and Honor

"Let everything that has breath praise the lord. Praise the Lord!"
Psalm 150:6 (NASB)

While watching the San Antonio Spurs win their first NBA Championship in 1999, I observed how the media frequently showed several demonstrations of celebration throughout the night. The streets were packed with people cheering, screaming, waving flags, and holding banners representing the Spurs.

At that moment, a question entered my mind: "How is it that we can effortlessly and publicly shout, cheer, and hold up banners for sports figures, teams, and entertainers? Why is it so difficult to do the same for Christ?" Such puzzling thoughts led me to write, "The Lord is My Banner."

"Moses built an altar and named it The Lord is My Banner."

Exodus 17:15 (NASB)

The Lord is My Banner

Rock of Salvation is He
Light of Life in me
Foundation of my soul
My Banner on a pole.

Represent! Represent!
In His Omnipotence!
A strong Deliverer is He
My Lord! My Conqueror—in me.

My Tour Guide through life
My Comforter of strife
O' Blessed is His name
For love is—His game.

My Father Internal!
My Life Eternal!
A bold soul witness this lamb
For the "Man—the great I AM!"

In the Bible, Jeremiah was a man on fire for God. The Book of Jeremiah continuously and passionately preaches to a nation who had lost their passion for God.

For those who believe in our Lord and Savior Jesus Christ and recognize all he has done for us through His death and resurrection, we must keep being on fire for God.

May our fire for Him burn night and day so that others may see the light of Jesus in our daily living.

On Fire For God

Inspired by Reverend Kevin D. Love

Are you on fire for God?
Does the fire for who He is—in you—still burn?
Or has your passion for him quietly burned out?

When met with discouraging words, negative attitudes,
And unsettling fears
Keep the fire of God's Word burning in your heart.
For the fire in Him—that burns for you—will never depart!

You must keep your desire to know Him and your passion for
experiencing his love flowing through your veins.
For His unjust death was evidence of His passion for you—
As he endured such excruciating pain.

When heartaches, pains, and disappointments
seem to never stop—
Do not let God's fiery flame of love—simply—burn out!
For His love—**Is still**—on fire for you.

It just keeps burning and burning—through and through.
Do not let anyone or anything extinguish your passion for Christ.

Just keep being "ON FIRE FOR GOD"
And
HE—will keep being ON FIRE FOR YOU!

"God said to Moses, I AM WHO I AM: and He said, 'Thus you shall say to the sons of Israel, I AM has sent me to you."

Exodus 3:14 (NASB)

The Great "I AM"

The Lord is the God of my Life
The King of my world.

The Light that lights my way
And thru it all—He lives—in me
And I am made in the image of Him.

He is the "I AM" of my life
My "sole" provider
Without Him I am incomplete.

For His name is "I AM"
And He is great.
For His power is eternal and His character
Never changes.

He is who He is—and—He is
The great "I AM!"

"And behold, you will conceive in your womb and bear a son, and you shall name him Jesus. He will be great and will be called the Son of the Most High; and the Lord God will give Him the throne of His father David."

"But the angel said to them, 'Do not be afraid; for behold, I bring you good tidings of great joy which will be for all the people; for today in the city of David there has been born for you a Savior, who is Christ the Lord . . ."

Luke 1:31, 32:10, 11 (NASB)

What's His Name?

Who is this man you speak of and what is his name?

Jesus is his name.

What you say?

Jesus . . . is his name!

How do you spell that?

J-----for **"JUST ENOUGH"**
E-----for **"ETERNAL LIFE"**
S-----for **"SON OF MAN"**
U-----for **"UNDENIABLE TRUTH"**
S -----for **"SAVIOR OF THE WORLD"**

JESUS!

Yes, that's His name.

DO YOU KNOW HIM?

When my niece Naysa was two years old, she and I were lovingly playing around in my mother's living room. Naysa wanted to do something, and not thinking, I said, "All right, whatever you want, Naysa. It's about you." Surprisingly, she turned around, pointed her finger at me, and responded, "No, Auntie Sheila! It's all about you!"

Needless to say, her words were unexpected. I thought to myself, "Lord, what a beautiful little creature you have allowed to be born . . . her birth is all about you."

You see, Naysa was born with the umbilical cord around her neck; if God had not directed things the way He did, Naysa might not be here today.

From that beautiful interaction with my niece and the circumstances which surrounded her birth, the poem, "It's All About You, Lord," was born.

It's All About You, Lord
Inspired by my beautiful niece, Naysa C. Kamau

When the sun rises in the East and sets in the West
And the seas flow from coast to coast
It's about you!

When there's no food to eat, and nothing but water to drink
Before the night is day—You have made a way.
It's about you, Lord!

When my enemies lie and connive behind my back
And friends and family deceive, betray, and disrespect me
My strength comes from you.

For you're the reason—Jesus
For all of life's seasons.

You're the reason why I can smile, and cry tears of joy,
And sing songs of praise.
You're the reason why I help others
Even when I have little for myself.
It's all about you!

Do you hear me Lord?

My spirit—is about You!
My striving to do better—is about You!
The times I step out of my place
And my desire to correct my mistakes. . .
It's about You, Lord!

The Courage . . . To Wake Up! To Rise Up!
To Continue on with Life!
To Love my Neighbors!
Speak kind words to Others!
It's About You!

My Obedience . . . To Honor my Mother and Father!
To Humble before You!
To Bow down to You!
To Praise Your Holy Name!
It's About You!

The Audacity . . . . .To Hope!
To be Joyful in spite of!
To Read Your Word!
Apply Your Word!
Share Your Word!
It's All About You Lord!

It's All about You!

So Thank You **Jesus**—for the "You" in "Me"
Because if it had not been for **You**—there would be no—**Me!**

Do you see Lord?—**It has to be--**

CONSTANTLY
CEASELESSLY
UNDENIABLY
And
MOST ASSUREDLY ABOUT YOU!

My Life Is All About You Lord!

"When I think of this, I fall to my knees and pray to the Father, the Creator of everything in heaven and on earth."

Ephesians 3:14, 15 (NLT)

The Work of the Creator

In the beginning was. . .
Conception—
Conceived in His mind
Formulated by Him.

—The **WORLD**—

It was! They were! We were!
Formed, shaped, and designed by him.
All things were brought into existence.

The **EARTH** and its **INHABITANTS**
HUMANS and **ANIMALS**
OCEANS and **SEAS**
FLOWERS and **TREES**
Even the **BIRDS** and **BEES**

This work of the Creator was and still is—His. . .

PHENOMENAL
EXTRAORDINARY
MOST REMARKABLE
UNMISTAKABLE
Truly **AUTHENTIC CREATION!**

Yes, **His Creation!**

The Lord our God. . .

CONCEIVED it!
INVENTED it!
PRODUCED it!
CREATED it!

This thing called **LIFE**

Being the Creator makes Him . . .

The **INVENTOR**
ORIGINATOR
PRODUCER
BUILDER
AUTHOR and **FINISHER**
Of everything that lives and breathes—from A-to-Z.

The work of the Creator—
Is an **EXTRAORDINARY** masterpiece
Created by the **MASTER!**

"The Lord sustains all who fall and raises up all who are bowed down. The eyes of all look to You, and You give them their food in due time. You open Your hand and satisfy the desire of every living thing."

Psalm 145:14-16 (NASB)

"Blessed be the God and Father of our Lord Jesus Christ, who has blessed us with every spiritual blessing in the heavenly places in Christ."

Ephesians 1:3 (NASB)

Who "He" Is . . .

Who is He?
This man whose name is constantly being called. . .

As a child, I heard my grandmother call His name.
As a youth, I heard my mother cry out His name.
As a woman, I call on His name.

Who is this man whose name is heard around the world?
Who everyone needs but many do not believe nor accept.

Do you know who He is?
Let me tell you just who He is.

He is. . .
Alpha and Omega
Savior and Lord
Everything begins and ends with Him.

He is. . .
Love, Patience, and Peace
Our breath of fresh air.

He is . . .
Bread of life
Sustainer and Deliverer
Redeemer and Forgiver of sins.

He is . . .
Hope and Joy
Light of the World
Sufficient Security and Protector in dangerous times.

He is . . .
Brother and Friend
One who will last to the very end.

Many call Him. . .
    "God the Father"

Some call Him. . .
    "God the Son"

Others call Him. . .
    "God the Holy Spirit"

But I call Them

"The HOLY TRINITY!"

That's who **"He"** is!

Motivation &
Spiritual Strength

"But those who trust in the Lord will find new strength. They will soar high on wings like eagles."

Isaiah 40:31 (NLT)

"Hope deferred makes the heart sick, but a dream fulfilled is a tree of life."

Proverbs 13:12 (NLT)

Follow Your Dream

Follow your dream
Even if sometimes you feel a sting.
Follow your dream
For in your dreams you are the queen or king.

When life
Sends you down a winding road
Follow your dream,
For at the end of the road
Is your pot of gold!

Follow your dream
Even when others try to stifle you—
And they will—

Just step back—take a deep breath—then exhale!
For it is your dream
And all the rest can go to . . . Well . . .

To follow your dream is your God given right
So guard your dream
And follow it—
By day and by night.

"Gently instruct those who oppose the truth. Perhaps God will change those people's hearts, and they will learn the truth. Then they will come to their senses and escape from the devil's trap . . ."

2 Timothy 2:25, 26 (NLT)

For Every New Level There's a New Devil

For every New Level
There's a New Devil.

For every New Position
You are met with Opposition.

For every New Transition
You have to make a New Decision.

And for every decision based
On Divine Instruction

There you have avoided
Satan's Destruction.

Aunt Hattie's Message

When I was in my late twenties, I had an aunt (my mother's sister) who I spent much time visiting. She was a very lovely and sweet Christian woman, who was full of life, knowledge, and wisdom.

I visited her often—simply to be in her presence. I loved her so much I just wanted to spend time with her. On this particular day she told me she wanted to tell me something that she did not ever want me to forget; it proved to be a profound message for me.

She said, "Sheila, I want you to always remember something." She went on to say, "I want you to learn how to give people their flowers while they are alive to enjoy them because it won't do them any good when they're gone." With a puzzled look on my face, I said, "Aunt Hattie, do you mean I have to buy people flowers all the time?" She said (with a huge grin on her face), "No, child! Just be kind and sincere in your giving! Give even the smallest of things! Do it spontaneously, and do it just because."

More importantly, "When you give, do it without expecting anything in return. And Baby, when you do this frequently and correctly . . . God recognizes your giving and there lies your reward!"

It has been several years since Aunt Hattie has gone on to be with the Lord, but her words of wisdom have proven to be true because they have left me with no regrets!

Giving Them Their Flowers Just Because
Inspired by and dedicated to Hattie M. King

Have you given someone their flowers today?
Have you shared a loving hug or sincere smile with someone recently?
Have you given a compliment where one is due?
Just Because. . .

Have you fed a hungry person today?
When was the last time you blessed someone that you didn't even know?
Or had words of encouragement for some lonely soul?
When was the last time you did these things?
Just Because. . .

When was the last time you told your children, parents, siblings and
Most intimate of friends—that you loved them—unconditionally?
How often have you put those words into action?
They say, "Action speaks louder than words."

To every niece and nephew,
When was the last time you took the opportunity to hold
Your auntie's hand?
Just because—You Can!

To all of God's children
This day I share Hattie's message with you.
A day <u>NOT</u> guaranteed to any of us.
Take the time—to let the **God in you shine**!

Give some unsuspecting soul their flowers today
For surely you will have shown-that in your life-God leads the way!

NO REGRETS!
NO REGRETS!

"There will be a shelter to give shade from the heat by day, and refuge and protection from the storm and the rain."

                                                    Isaiah 4:6 (NASB)

Pushing Past Your Storms

When the storms of life have knocked you down
Don't stop fighting your way through,
Keep pushing past your storms!

When people say they "love you" but
Physically and emotionally hurt you—don't get angry.

JUST KEEP PUSHING!

When friends or loved ones can no longer be there for you
Don't get mad or sad—You may not know the reasons why.

Maybe you've been relying too much on family and friends
Instead of relying on yourself and utilizing the gifts and tools
That God has equipped you with.

Gifts and tools—to maneuver through this life
And the storms and rains it brings.

When driving down life's road and you run into a storm
DON'T STOP!

Keep on pushing and driving through the rain—if you stop
You set yourself up to stay in the rain.

When the storms of life hinders your ability to see clearly
DON'T STOP!

Keep pushing past the storm, past the rain, and past the pain
Because if you stop then you have chosen
To get—

Caught up and stuck in—Your storm!
Your rain! And your pain!
And God did not design you for that!

He made you, created you, designed you, and built you
To push past the storms, the rains, and the pains!

Because you are His child and **HIS** children **DO NOT**
Sit, waddle, or linger in storms of negativity.

We stand up!
We push through! We drive through!
And we get through!

Because storms will never cease to come
But if you keep on pushing through
When you look back. . .

You'll find that you have left yet another STORM BEHIND!

Then when you look up to the clear blue sky
The rainbow covenant you will see.

That's God's promise to you
Of just where He will always be. . .

LIVING INSIDE OF YOU
and
PUSHING YOU PAST YOUR STORMS!

Like spinach was to Popeye, faith is to a child of God. It nourishes our body with the spiritual substance we need to run the Christian race.

"You don't have enough faith," Jesus told them. "I tell you the truth, if you had faith even as small as a mustard seed, you could say to this mountain, 'Move from here to there,' and it would move. Nothing would be impossible."

Matthew 17:20 (NLT)

"For whatever is born of God overcomes the world: and this is the victory that has overcome the world—our faith."

1 John 5:4 (NASB)

Feed Your Faith-Starve Your Doubts

Feeding your faith and starving your doubts requires
A life changing attitude.
When a mother feeds her children she is …

PROVIDING for them
NOURISHING their bodies
And giving them **SUBSTANCE** to **SUSTAIN** them.

Does God do the same for His children?

Yes! He **provided** for us when
He gave man dominion over the land.
He **nourished** our bodies when He gave us His "Holy Word" to eat
365 days of the year, and 366 days on leap year.
He gave us eternal **substance**
When He gave us His "only begotten Son—Christ Jesus,"
A life-**sustaining food**.

So when you are feeling hungry—go find your food of faith,
and feed it with the Word of God.

When you continually feed your faith—you feed—

Your **TRUST** in Him
Your **CONFIDENCE** in who He is
Your **ASSURANCE** that He lives in you
Your **CONVICTION** that He is who He says "He Is"
Your **ACCEPTANCE** that He alone is the ONE & ONLY true
SAVIOR.

By constantly feeding your faith, you starve that doubt of . . .

CHRIST'S EXISTENCE
That **UNCERTAINTY** of who He is
You stop **QUESTIONING** His love for you
You become **CONVINCED** that He is who He says "He Is"
You stop **WONDERING** if He lives in you.

When you **FEED YOUR FAITH** and **STARVE YOUR DOUBTS**
You experience an everlasting
LIFE CHANGING ATTITUDE!

"God is not unjust; he will not forget your work and the love you have shown him as you have helped his people and continue to help them."

Hebrews, 6:10 (NIV)

Significant Life of a Christian Woman

SIGNIFICANT!
    MEANINGFUL!
        IMPORTANT!
            NOTABLE!
                VITAL!

Is the life of a true Christian woman!
One that requires a change of attitude!

For the significant life of a Christian woman is
A life that has experienced
The awesome touch of the Master's Hands.

She is described as. . .

BEAUTIFUL!
    WISE!
        GRACIOUS!
            HONORABLE!
                And
                    HOLY!

Her life's work consists of. . .

Kneading. *. . the dough that feeds her family*
Drawing. *. . . the water that quenches their thirst*
Tending. *. . .to the matters of the heart and spirit*
Nurturing. *. . .the lives of her children*
Caring. *. . .for her household*
And the household that extends beyond her four walls.

Her Godly position is. . .

God's creation. *. . .from Man*
And His helper. *. . .to Man.*

But her spiritual position encompasses . . .

ENDLESS SERVITUDE!
CONTINUAL PRAYER!
UNCONDITIONAL UNDERSTANDING!
CONSTANT LABORING!

Her **FAITH** *and* **WISDOM** *are profoundly, sincerely, and deeply rooted in Christ!*

They say. . .her good and Godly traits are those of. . .
OBEDIENCE!
TENDERNESS!
LOYALTY!
MODESTY!
And
COMPLETE DEVOTION to her **LORD!**

For her "life" is the righteous, the glorious, and holy product
That has been divinely touched by "her" Master's hands.

A Godly touch that demands a change of attitude!

For that she is loved
And
HER LIFE IS SIGNIFICANT!

Inspiration Through Spiritual Journeys

"He renews my strength. He guides me along right paths, bring honor to his name."

Psalm 23:3

This poem reminds me of my Mother. I grew up listening to her sing spiritual hymns and gospel songs every day. She has been singing praises to and for the Lord since before my birth.

Everyone always asks, "How does that little woman sing with such a powerful voice?" I always say, "It is because she believes in what she is singing about and who she is singing for."

When I see and listen to my Mother sing in the choir, I always feel like I am the proud mother; I want to shout, "That's my Mama!" I get such a glorious feeling when I see the Holy Spirit move through her and when I witness how her spiritual light brings joy to the congregation.

I am very proud of all that she has accomplished. **Mother, your voice will always be the song in my heart . . . I love you.**

"...Sing psalms and hymns and spiritual songs to God with thankful hearts. And whatever you do or say, do it as a representative of the Lord Jesus, giving thanks through him to God the Father."
Colossians 3:16, 17(NLT)

The Light of Energy Through Spiritual Praise

Through spiritual light is spiritual energy revealed—
Being of His creation and in the image of Him
Thus dwell His light within.

O' happy am I when singing His praises
For a great songstress I am not-but only to Him.

To Him who hears the melody in my heart
Who sees the light that dwells within my soul,
O' great is He who ignites my fire.

Personal is this relationship of love—by choice,
And sacred is this bond of friendship—eternal.

Oh! Let His light shine through me for all to see
For full is my cup and it runneth over.

Gather together, you who know Him, and sing His praises
Through song, instruments, raising of holy hands, stomping of holy
feet, and through our daily living.

Lift Him up in Spirit and let His internal light shine
throughout our gathering, thus creating a spiritual energy eternal!

The following poetic trilogy was written to friends as spiritual encouragement and inspiration, as they traveled through their personal journeys. I pray also that they will be an encouragement to you.

"Your testimonies also are my delight; They are my counselors."
Psalms 119:24 (NASB)

Along This Journey

On this winding road that you have ventured down
You have stumbled, fallen, and tumbled to the ground.
But in your pain you didn't give up, you didn't give in,
You just became determined to rise again.

Rise my friend! Rise! Rise! And Rise again!
For you are a pillar of strength even in your weakest moment.
Along this journey you have met many strangers
Because of your love they are strangers no more.

Your warmth, your kindness, and your
Willingness to teach—with God's blessings
Many souls you have reached.

—Along this journey—

You have been a teacher of students and a comforter to the end
A mother to children, and even your friends.
In the end, you have been God's blessed child
Following His instructions, mile after mile.

—Along this journey—

Can you see? God has appointed you our honoree!

To give back to you what you have given to us
Oh, my dear, I'm sorry—we could never give enough.

—Along this journey—

Our paths have now crossed but will never end.
It's been fun! It's been real!
But now, your new journey begins . . .

"Who can find a virtuous and capable wife? She is more precious than rubies. Her husband can trust her, and she will greatly enrich his life. She brings him good, not harm, all the days of her life."

Proverbs 31:10-12 (NLT)

The Heart of a Pastor's Wife

The heart of a pastor's wife is strategically created
And designed by God in a meticulous kind of way.
It is uniquely designed and planted
In a "particular" kind of woman—

Long before she ever knows that she will marry a preacher,
God carefully designed her to be a woman of strength, courage,
And patience, guided by a gentle and loving heart.

He knew—she would need all of those attributes just to run this
Christian race alongside God's appointed servant, who we call Pastor.
God knew she had to be a woman whose heart and soul
Would show forth a strong character,
Deep wisdom and a great compassion for others.
She is skillful in much.

He created that kind of heart in her–this woman of God,
A kind of heart that shows in all she says and does,
And throughout the many lives she touches.
Woman of God—this heart in you—I do commend!
This is the Heart of a Pastor's Wife

In her obedience to the Lord, she puts her husband, and shepherd of
The flock before all—his health, well-being, and finances –
His home, his heart, and Godly call.
This is the heart of a Pastor's Wife

She has learned to love the flock he leads, just as he does.
She gracefully and willingly shares him with family, friends,
And so many others, while having little time with him for herself.
This too is the heart of a Pastor's Wife

She always has beautiful smiles and encouraging words
Awaiting all who come in her presence.
She continually shows compassion by helping the needy,
Listening, and inspiring the hurt and lost.
If her husband and pastor is on call 24 hours a day
She—the pastor's wife—is on call 24 hours a day.
When he is troubled, or faced with oppositions
In his vision for the church—
After the Lord, she is his comfort and strength.
This too is the heart of a Pastor's Wife

She prays with him and for him.
She willingly follows his lead
So long as it is Jesus he is following.
Her strength, dignity, and integrity come from her sincere love
And deep reference for God.
She alone has been wonderfully, awesomely
And strategically created
For this significant and lonely, but critical position!

She is carefully and magnificently designed
By the hands of the Master for this most heavenly position
That is why she has been specifically chosen to receive
The "heart" of a Pastor's Wife.

"Speaking to one another in psalms and hymns and spiritual songs, singing and making melody with your heart to the Lord."

Ephesians 5:19 (NASB)

A Humbling Experience

Sitting in church one day
I heard a musical sound
Ratta-tat-tat! One-two-three
Goes the twinkling of the
Black and white keys.

Upon my glance there was a woman
On the piano in deep conversation
She spoke to God as she stroked the piano chords
With great synchronization.

What a humbling experience to see those anointed fingers flow.

Before she could ever utter a word
The Holy Spirit spoke with each touch of the keys
While every divine sound floated through the air
Like a cool summer's breeze.

Listening to the beautiful music she was making
We watched her fingers move across the piano
Like the wind moves across a stream.
She generated spirit-filled ripples in the atmosphere
So that all could take time to dream.

When her heart is full and has much to say
She sits at the piano and let her fingers have their way.
Her dedicated fingers and those ivory keys bring forth
Such heavenly music that transcends
Far above the tallest of trees.

Sheila R. McElroy

With her spirit-filled heart and anointed fingers
She goes where others dare not linger.
To that secret place where only she resides
With her heavenly Father right by her side.

A humbling experience indeed.

PoetryNMotion

The following pages are for you to have your personal conversation with God. Write it down, so you will be able to reflect on it when He responds to your prayer.

If this book has blessed you in some way, please share it with me through my Author pages at www.barnesandnoble.com and www.amazon.com

NOTES
Reflections and Conversations with God

Questions:

1. Do you believe God seeks an intimate relationship with you? If so, why?

2. Has God spoken to you through these poetic inspirations?

3. If the above answer is yes, then what do you believe God is asking of you, and how do you plan to respond?

    Do you desire to have an intimate relationship with God? If so, then pray about it, and let the Lord know that you desire to be closer to Him. Speak to Him on a daily basis, confess everything. Be patient and listen for His voice – it will come.

NOTES
Reflections and Conversations with God

NOTES
Reflections and Conversations with God

NOTES
Reflections and Conversations with God

NOTES
Reflections and Conversations with God

NOTES
Reflections and Conversations with God

www.ingramcontent.com/pod-product-compliance
Lightning Source LLC
Chambersburg PA
CBHW032028040426
42448CB00006B/766